HOW TO GET RICH THIS YEAR

By

HARSHHAA GARG

Pendown Press

Powered by Gullybaba.com

"Money is like oxygen for your life and is available in abundance. However, you live in the suffocation of limited supply of money around you because of some misconceptions about the world of Money. It is your duty to resolve these misconceptions and live in the truth about Getting Rich and the truth is, Getting Rich is your birth right and with more money, you live lively and serve more."

–Harshhaa Garg

CONTENTS

WHO MUST READ THIS BOOK

Would you love to live your life with dignity?

Would you love to live your life with all the essentials of life?

Would you love to live your life with all the luxuries in your life?

Would you love to live your life as you always dream?

If the answer of any of the questions mentioned above is yes, this mini book is certainly for you. I have put all the nectars in this book that I could gather after travelling extensively across the length and breadth of India and abroad, spending millions, meeting with hundreds of influential people, attending hundreds of seminars, hobnobbing with several persons who have made their presence felt in their respective fields. It cost me lots of mental and physical pain in the form of expenses, losses, travel, struggling to figure out what's working and what's not working. I travelled a long way to discover a life of abundance. The path was never easy. It was full of thorns, challenges, difficulties, failure at times. I took all the pains so that I can help you get painless journey and sure shot success.

I have tried to explain every point in this book in a very simple manner to make things super easy for you so that you don't have to put extra effort to understand certain things. I have also tried to address following self-limiting beliefs which stop you from achieving your dream of Getting Rich:

- You think money is something you will get in your next birth.
- You think money is not coming your way because of the sins of your past births.
- You think money is for business class and you are certainly not in that class.
- You think that you are fortunate not to have money, for if money comes to you, then you may not remain the person you are, because money always brings vices.
- You think you have tried everything possible to get rich, however failed to get money.
- You curse your fate when money does not flow as expected in your business.

With my mini book, I want to ensure that you will not experience the lack, if you read this book avidly. This short book will help you even more, because the sooner you get to know about the Mechanism of Money, the better it is. If you pick this short book and make a habit to read it daily, you will yourselves feel the benefit that you got some years down the line.

I have tried my level best to incorporate all those things which are essential in the quest of money making, despite knowing about the page constraints. This booklet is exclusively written for you, hence it is incumbent on you to enlighten me about any suggestion that you may have for the betterment of its content. I will be very happy to have your suggestion. In my next edition, I will incorporate all those suggestions that merit inclusion.

MY STORY

A number of years ago I was doing very well in my corporate career. But, I was not at peace with my inner self. I would feel myself torn between my job and the inner turbulence. I was vying for something remarkable in my life which I was not getting in my life. When I used to be at office, there was no excitement of going back my home, and when I was at home, I was not willing to go to office. The thought of quitting job crossed my mind several times. But, it was not an easy decision after all.

Let me ask, have you ever had similar feelings in your job when you just wanted to quit? Tell me a little about that experience.

I quit my job. But then I realised that how I had no love and respect for Money in the true sense. I was doing that job only to satisfy my ego that I am independent and I don't need my father's money to enjoy little luxuries of life. That was my mistake and I learnt that what we nurture and care for, grows rapidly.

What are the things you nurture and care so deeply in your life? Notice how it is growing in your life.

As a child, I was born and brought up in an abundant family. I had almost everything I could have thought of having as a child. Whenever there was a need of anything, I would ask for it to my father, and I would get it almost instantly. I would get money without telling much about why I need it. I was getting money as pocket money, for celebrating birthdays, getting new gadgets, for shopping, etc. My parents would send me for school tour, school picnic, etc. with quite good amount of money.

Have you or any of your childhood friends had a happy-go-lucky childhood like mine? Tell me what do you feel about your childhood money experiences?

This was great as a child; however, all these abundance took a toll on my thinking about money. I failed to understand the importance of money and had no sense of gratitude for my father for providing for my desires and I was taking it all for granted. I remember I would never look for a dropped pen, pencil, or even expensive things; for I knew that getting these things new is just one information away. All that I needed to get a new item in place of an old one was to inform my parents that I lost my……

Since I was getting money without any effort, I made a perception that having money is not a big thing and so who possess it, does not need any special regard. Whenever I used to get money from my relative, an attitude of gratitude was missing on my face. I was taking these things for granted.

I think this is where I made a big mistake. I took the source of abundant energy, *i.e.,* money very lightly. And it will not be a hyperbole to say that for this misconception, I had to pay heavily in my prime. Lesson learned the hard way, *"Never take anything for granted, learn to appreciate what you have, before it's no longer yours to appreciate."*

Let me ask, what all you are taking for granted in your life? Who are the people/things you are not appreciative of and how it is impacting your experience of life?

A few years ago when I started my entrepreneurial journey, I saw the other side of the table as an employer, where money is first going out from my side in the form of salaries, office expenses and if something is left then I can get my salary. I was investing my savings in it and would see my savings balance getting reduced and at times I would even borrow from my father. This situation wasn't a great situation to be in—it was impacting my self-respect, confidence and was crippling me with the thought of financial insecurity.

Have you ever felt these financial insecurities and low confidence in yourself? Tell me about your money challenges when you started your entrepreneurial journey? What did you do to overcome those challenges?

After a few months of being in this situation, I started asking this question from myself, how people make a lot of money and freedom around money? I invested lakhs of rupees in last 8 years to learn from the best masters in the world on this subject by reading their books and participating in their trainings and 1-2-1 coaching.

I realised that Money is a learnable skill and can be mastered with practice. You can always make sure that money is well invested and taken good care of. Likewise, you can change the way you think about the persons having lots of money.

Now, I want to share these learning with you so that you can live a Rich life of ease, joy and love with Money, living your passions while enjoying your work.

> *"Harshhaa gives a magic wand to the reader that can change their perception of life and convert dreams into reality with the 20 Golden Secrets of How to Get Rich. Reading and inculcating the powerful motivating message given by her in the book, one would have tryst with destiny."*
>
> ***–Aman Agarwal,***
>
> *Professor & Director, Indian Institute of Finance and Executive Editor, Finance India*

THE TRUTH ABOUT GETTING RICH

Getting Rich is your birth right and with abundance of money, you live lively and serve more.

Let's begin the journey of getting rich by first getting aware about your Money perception. Interestingly, everyone perceives money differently. A dollar may be insignificant to one, but precious to another. *How does the understanding of money evolved in every individual's mind?*

Through the years of growing up, nobody gave you a 'how to use money' guide, there isn't any academic subjects on personal money management either. You picked up money habits from people around, your siblings, your best friends, your social cliques, guru from some financial seminars that you attended, the news channels, social media, etc. Your schools, communities and associations have a set of culture that shaped your money belief system. And even religious teaching may have certain values on finances.

Given below is a set of questions, I want answer from you. I know my different set of readers will have different answers. The reason for this test, I will disclose later. Right now, let me have a Reality Check on your perceptions regarding money.

1. Money for you is…

(a) Root cause of all evils

(b) Necessary evil

(c) Source of livelihood, but not something to appreciate

(d) Is source of living with gratitude and grace

2. People who get Money

(a) Become addictive of it

(b) Start devaluating people

(c) Squander money

(d) May not necessarily be of bad nature

3. You think that the Process of Getting Rich is

(a) Dishonest Means

(b) Doing lots of business together

(c) Deceive people

(d) Desire for money, Perseverance

4. Which of the following is required to be Rich?

(a) Being Comfortable with Taking Risks

(b) Being Visionary

(c) Having high self confidence

(d) All of the above

5. If I get more and more Money...

(a) I will become heartless

(b) I will become unmindful of the self-respect of people

(c) My very purpose of helping people will be defeated

(d) I will be able to do lots of welfare to the people

6. I am content with what amount of Money I have because…

(a) If I get more, I will not be the same person

(b) Moneyed becomes unprincipled

(c) Moneyed becomes unethical

(d) I want to get more and more money through ethical ways

7. Money does not come alone; it brings lots of…

(a) Adversity

(b) Vices

(c) Bad relationship

(d) Good things

8. I do not like Money because…

(a) I know how money can be a bad master

(b) I know how money turns to be devastating if not controlled

(c) I think money brings negativity

(d) I do like money

9. The Rich know

(a) How to ditch people

(b) How to harvest the misfortune of others

(c) How to earn money without actually working

(d) How to turn adversities into opportunities

10. I do not respect moneyed because

(a) They become haughty/proud

(b) They demoralise poor

(c) They make super image about themselves

(d) I respect money/moneyed

If most of your answers are (d), it means your perception about money is right. If it is not (d), you need to introspect.

The right perception about money in respect of the following three states is the first step:

i. **What is "Money" for you?**

ii. **What it means to be "Rich?"**

iii. **How you relate to the "Process of Getting Rich"**

If you at all think that the Rich might have achieved financial abundance through ill means, you should change your thinking pattern and bring positivity in your way of thinking. You can see interviews of business tycoons and come to know about their struggle and how did they turn their adversities into opportunities. You can read various articles, books etc. about the successful and wealthy people of this world who did not become the persons they are by chance, but by sheer tenacity and out-of-box thinking.

Tell me the name of the successful and wealthy person whose story inspired you lately.

If you also want to start your Path of Prosperity, you have to be prudent spender, develop the tendency to save, build a project from scratch and be ready to take risks. Other must-have qualities include being visionary, displaying confidence, being assertive, saying no and doing what others dither to do.

I invite you to change the equation in your mind as per below:

Money=Necessary Evil and Disturbances	Necessary to live life with Dignity and with Opportunities
Rich=Greed and Corrupt	Kind and heart-warming individuals
Process of Getting Rich= Hard and Uncomfortable	Fun, Comfortable and Rewarding

If you live with limiting beliefs about MONEY, you will keep on negating abundance opportunities into your life. Remember, your MIND IS VERY POWERFUL. It records all your thoughts, beliefs, and then translates these and put in front of your life to experience in real world. Now, it is up to you.

Do you want to fill your mind with all the negativities related with money and live a deprived life, or entertain your mind with thought of abundance and prove to be an asset for your family, friends, relatives and society?

With the right perception about money, the next step is to have 100% faith in your right to be rich and 100% commitment to take all the necessary actions now to realise and enjoy this right to the fullest in your life.

When you focus on end result, and let your faith work, you will be directed towards specific people, circumstances and opportunities which will make your journey smooth. So, if you want richness to land at your way, you will need to build the airport of faith.

Finally, you decide to be rich, you don't take no for an answer and don't give up. You are committed to be Rich, you are not treating "getting rich" as a hobby, or something that you'll just try out and see what happens. It doesn't work that way. Remember, Time and Tide wait for none, so this is the best time to act, do whatever is possible and necessary and make your dream, a reality. There are some cogent reasons why I tell you that NOW is the best time. Some of these are mentioned below:

- **Better be uncomfortable today than regret later:** You are no longer a kid. You cannot cry, if someone forbids you to play your favourite game. You should not be in search of your favourite game. Rather, you should have the ability to make every game of yours, your favorite. When you do this you train your mind to do the things which are uncomfortable on the face of it.
- **Those who keep showing up rather than becoming complacent are the ones who get Rich:** Irrespective of the level of richness, those who keep showing up are the ones who climb the ladder of Money game. It is the time, not to get affected by your achievements, be it possessions, recognition or luxuries. With so many possessions, many become boastful and power drunk and start to show-off or become complacent

and that's when instead of going ahead towards the destination of getting rich, they rather go backwards in the game of Money. Those who do not show off, remain humble and show-up whenever they can add value in their own capacity, become able to get closer to the destination of Getting Rich.

Always ask yourself, is this the best investment I can make off with my Time, Health, Relationships and Money to move forward in my journey of Getting Rich? If the answer is yes, then move ahead else leave it as another shiny object that is trying to distract you from your path of Getting Rich. It's like the time in hand today is the time you will never have tomorrow so make the best of it and achieve your dream of Getting Rich.

20 GOLDEN SECRETS I LEARNT ABOUT GETTING RICH

1. **Rich Mind-set:** A mind-set that loves RICH and believes in the richness of everything. The term Rich mind-set pertains to the ability to reframe the words you use for every favourable or not-so-favourable experience of your life to that of Richness. A mind-set that thinks ahead of the time and takes maximum use of an opportunity to be rich, without taking anybody else's right to be Rich.

> *"It's not the load that breaks you down, it's the way you carry it."*
>
> ***–Lou Holtz,***
>
> *American football player, coach and analyst*

> *"I have not failed; I have just found 10,000 ways that don't work."*
>
> ***–Thomas Edison,***
>
> *American Inventor and Businessman*

2. **Hangout with Rich:** We are the average of five people we spend our time with. Everything has energy. So to become rich, hangout with Rich so that their energy rubs on you and you by default start perceiving the thoughts and behaviour of the Rich.

> *"We become like the people we associate with."*
>
> ***–Steve Siebold,***
>
> *Self-made millionaire and author of How Rich People Think*

3. **Patience:** Patience is Gold on the path of becoming Rich. Nature is the biggest example of learning patience. Nature does not hurry, yet everything is accomplished. Germination is a must for a seed to get transformed into plant and then fruit.

> *"It took me 17 years and 114 days to become an overnight success. Be patient."*
>
> ***–Lionel Messi,***
> *Argentine professional footballer*

> *"Trust the process. Your time is coming. Just do the work and the results will handle themselves."*
>
> ***–Tony Gaskins,***
> *Motivational speaker, author and life coach*

4. **Shower yourself with Self Love**: Truly Rich are those who love themselves as they are the ones who enjoy and celebrate every moment, be it good or not-so-good, of their life. We are the source of our richness so when we love ourselves, we give our best effort for anything we are doing on our path to Get Rich.

> *"Love yourself first and everything else falls in line. You really have to love yourself to get anything done in this world."*
>
> ***–Lucille Ball,***
> *American Actress*

5. **Focus on Serving with One thing which gives you money:** Identify how you are helping people who are giving you money currently. Once identified, focus on building it up and create enough corpuses from it, before you diversify your energy into other things. Remember, everything takes energy and everything takes maintenance, so choose for yourself that one thing you want to focus on your energy to Get Rich.

> *"Capitalize on what comes."*
>
> *–ZigZiglar ,*
> *American Author, salesman, speaker*

6. **Always Value your Time and utilise it in the most efficient manner:** Always remember that Time is Money. In fact, time is the most expensive currency in the world as once you have spent your time on something you cannot get that time back, it is gone forever. It is a non-renewable resource provided in limited quantity to

each one of us. On the other side, if we make some monetary loss in a deal, we can still have a chance to recover it through another good deal. Thus, Money is a renewable resource. With this understanding, practise being a conscious investor of your time, the one who enjoys the play with time on his path to Get Rich.

> *"Time is really the only capital that any human being has, and the only thing he can't afford to lose."*
>
> ***–Thomas Edison,***
>
> *American Inventor and Businessman*

7. **Always add more value than the money exchange:** Whatever be your product/service, always be mindful of operating from adding higher value than the money value of your product/service. This way you win the heart of your customer and serve the ultimate purpose of your product/service. Always be more, do more and serve more to Get Rich.

> *"I'd rather be the jester who adds value to those around me than a King with no vision or intention of making a difference."*
>
> ***–Janna Cachola,***
>
> *New Zealand based actress, singer*

8. **Connect with the source of abundance to serve more:** Remember, nature is bountiful and there is enough for everyone's needs on this planet, but not enough to cater to the limitless wants which results into greed and an experience of scarcity of resources. Abundance refers to having plenty of time, freedom and ability to do with confidence whatever positive you wish to do and achieve. Develop your love, respect and connection with the ultimate source of abundance, *i.e.*, divine universal energy and live every moment in experience of all abundance and Get Rich.

> *"You can become instantly successful with a simple thought, but long-lasting and pronounced success comes to those who renew their commitment to a mind-set of abundance every minute of every hour of every day."*
>
> ***–Bryant McGill,***
> *Human potential thought leader, author and social entrepreneur*

9. **Educate yourself on the Basics of Money:** Many people struggle on their path to Richness because they don't understand the very basics of Money. Money is the energy which is known as currency and it flows. It never likes hoarding. Many people make the mistake by trying to hold the money. This is a big roadblock on their path to get rich. Become a joyful space/channel for money energy to flow through you to Get Rich.

> *"Earning a lot of money is not the key to prosperity. How you handle it is."*
>
> ***–Dave Ramsey,***
> *American author and businessman*

10. **Money Loves Attention:** Money is like any other human being in our life. The way our children, friends, spouse needs our love and attention to be with us, in the same way money needs our love and attention to be with us. Pay attention to money by tracking it, the more you track your money both coming in and out, the more you'll find yourself moving up the ladder of achieving your goal of Getting Rich.

> *"Where attention goes energy flows and results show."*
>
> *–T. HarvEker,*
> *Author of international best seller,*
> *Secrets of a millionaire mind*

11. **Leverage all the Resources:** Learn how to leverage all the resources in your hand, be it people, technology, an event, etc. In every favourable or not-so-favourable moment of your life look at it as a lever be provided to you by GOD and see what you can do to lift yourself up using this lever and then do that and Get Rich.

    The purpose of a lever is to pull a heavy weight in a manner as if it is a light weighted needle rising high.

12. **Design and Play your own Game, the one you know you can win:** Many people are distracted by the glitter of far off things for which they have very little or no

knowledge at all. They start chasing it at the cost of close-by things or things in which they have almost all the knowledge or expertise. This is one of the most common mistakes by all the people who are trying for long to Get rich and still haven't reached and have no clue how and by when they will ever reach.

Let me ask you, what game are you playing? Is it the right game for your particular skills and talents? Is it a perfect set-up for you or your company to win? If not, then perhaps it's time to play a different game or invent one of your own; one that you can win.

> *"Everyone is a genius, but if you judge a fish on its ability to climb a tree, it will live its whole life believing that it is stupid."*
>
> ***–Albert Einstein,***
>
> *German-born Physicist and Nobel prize winner*

> *"If you play to your strengths, you'll turn in a superior performance. Just be yourself."*
>
> ***–Yuki Kure,***
>
> *Japanese manga artist, illustrator and an author*

13. **Develop the Foresight to Study Patterns and Predict Future:** Everything around us has a pattern in which it flows. For instance, stock market has a pattern that gets repeated almost every ten years, your spouse has a behavioural pattern, and your parents have a behavioural pattern. So, when you do a deep study of happenings around you, then you will be able to see these patterns for your business/profession, investment trends, and thereby will be able to capitalise on what comes in your way. Simply put, this is an advanced skill in the game of getting rich.

> *"The world is giving you answers each day, learn to listen."*
>
> *-Anonymous*

14. **Master the art of organising people who have certain talent:** Most of the people have become Rich through the channel of business and you can also get rich through this channel. Business as a channel to Get Rich requires one to master the art of organising people with a certain talent in a smoothly flowing machine which works 24/7 even without you. If you master this art, rest assured, getting rich will certainly be a reality in your life.

> *"The only difference between a mob and a trained army is organisation."*
>
> **–Calvin Coolidge,**
> *30th US president*

15. **Enjoy the Game of Money:** In the game of money, you play with the world from the spirit of sportsmanship and are comfortable with profits and loss. When you make profits you enjoy, relish, celebrate your win and when you make losses you take it with ease as part of the game and don't lose your sight. You keep yourself grounded in both, profit/loss phases of the game of money and this is very important as this is the only way you will remain in the game. If you do not enjoy the game of money, you will soon quit and will be out of the game of getting Rich.

> *"Be it a money game or other games, only those win the game who play it with playing spirit and not get perturbed with success or failure. Quitters never win."*
>
> **–Anonymous**

16. **Develop a Knack of Identifying Opportunities to Invest:** This channel to get rich requires one to build the financial discipline of saving and acumen of investing. This channel has been adopted by the likes of Warren Buffet, who has built all his wealth through investments in the stock markets. Any individual can adopt this channel, however this requires one to learn the science of investment and discipline to save at least 20% of your income every month and starting a disciplined investments early in life. Therefore, just get mastery over this art and Get Rich.

> *"Someone is sitting in the shade today because someone planted a tree long time ago."*
>
> ***-Warren Buffet,***
>
> *Chairman and CEO of Berkshire Hathaway*

17. **Know what a Real Asset is and Build it:** An asset is something/someone which feeds you which means it puts money in your pocket and a liability is something/someone which eats you which means it takes money out of your pocket. Many people are blinded by the number of possessions, be it materialistic things or number of office staff, friends or customers in their life. They are not able to segregate them into the two categories, if it is an asset or a liability. Most of the time

it is seen that 90% of the possessions one has are liabilities eating away their precious time and money. Commit to own Assets and get rid of Liabilities, and Get Rich.

> *"You must know the difference between an asset and a liability and, buy assets."*
>
> ***–Robert Kiyosaki,***
> *American businessman*
> *and author of Rich Dad Poor Dad*

18. **Conscious Spending is Rich Spending:** There are countless cases of people who are earning very well and are still not in the experience of being Rich. The reason is that they are spending their money unconsciously on anything and everything irrespective of their needs, wants and desires. Every dollar of your money is to be treated with love, respect and put to use consciously. So, get the diagnosis done if you are suffering from this disease and take the pill of Conscious Spending to Get Rich.

> *"The analysation of your spending habits is key to your financial success."*
>
> ***–Neela Okuromade,***
>
> *Finance Coach, Speaker and Author of the Book Series what's Your Financial Game plan*

19. **Negotiate your Deals and Tap into the Hidden Income:** Every month we consume so much and settle those bills in our personal as well as professional life. *Do you negotiate the bill or fear to negotiate?* Negotiating the deal for a better price or for a better package in a manner whereby both the seller and the buyer are at a win-win position because of the negotiation rather than a win-lose is another skill which is rarely found. By mastering the art of negotiation, you can add a sparkle to your journey to Get Rich.

> *"Let us never negotiate out of Fear.*
> *But let us never fear to Negotiate."*
>
> ***–John F Kennedy,***
>
> *Former American President*

> *"Treat negotiation as a partner-dance where the lead-follow roles are switched frequently in order to arrive at a win-win solution in a harmonious way."*
>
> ***–Anonymous***

20. **Be Responsible for your own Richness:** The mistake we do is that we want to Get Rich but are not willing to take the required inspired action to Get Rich. Nothing worthwhile is ever achieved without putting the required efforts.

> *"The one thing that you have that nobody else has is YOU, your voice, your mind, your story, your vision. So write and draw and build and play and dance and live as only you can."*
>
> ***–Neil Gaiman,***
> *English author of short fiction,*
> *comic books, audio theatre, and films*

20 Golden secrets I learnt about Getting Rich

THE FORMULA TO GET RICH

The formula to realise the desire to Get Rich is:

Rich Thoughts + Rich Feelings + Rich Actions = Get Rich ($$$)

The great among the greatest scientist Einstein once said, *"Whenever I think of Almighty, I find Him Mathematician, not magician."*

Very true, just as Mathematics, there are certain laws that must be abided by and the results can be tremendous with certainty. There is a science behind getting rich.

~~The chances are 2+2 will be four~~

2+2 will always be four.

TWO BONUS SECRETS TO GET RICH

I. Creative Visualisation

Creative visualisation is the process of using your thought power to consciously imagine, create and attract to yourself that which you intend to experience in your life. Visualisation happens to be one of the most effective tools to Get Rich. There are five basic steps to visualising your intentions for reality creation: Relax–Imagine–Feel–Believe–Detach.

Practice is the Key: You must practice, practice and practice. Set aside a time each day for your creative visualisations, preferably once in the morning upon waking and once at night before you go to sleep. Both these times are ideal as your mind is already in a semi-relaxed state. Once you have mastered this simple five step process, you will see your life transforming in miraculous ways.

Leave the How up to the Universe: The focus of your visualisations must be on the outcome, not the process. Once you accept the truth about your thought power and that you are one with the One Universal Mind, you will be able to release any need to control the process. Instructing the all-knowing Universe "how" you want things to come about is telling Omniscience that you know better.

Take Inspired Action: Although the creative visualisation process is based on relaxation, physical action is required to successfully manifest your mental intentions. The key to taking action is to take only inspired action. This is not to sit and wait for the proverbial penny to drop, nor is it to run around in a frenzied state doing everything you can possibly think of doing in the hope that something works. It is about being calm and deliberate in the action you take, knowing that it is taking you towards your intended outcome. It is about listening to your intuition and following your natural instinct.

In a nutshell, creative visualisation is the fundamental process underlying your innate ability to consciously create your ideal reality. The five steps you must master in visualising are to relax, imagine, feel and believe you already have that which you have mentally chosen and then detach yourself from the outcome you intend to see manifest in your life. After you have completed the visualization process, preferably twice a day, get on with the rest of your day. Leave the how up to the all-knowing Universal Mind and commit yourself to taking inspired action towards your intended outcome.

II. Attitude of Gratitude

Abundance in Gratitude Equals Abundance in Life. It's a simple formula that will transform your life. Say it out loud, write it down, think it, feel it, breathe it. Feel thankful for every step that you take. Stop focusing on the problems, focus on the solution. And the solution is simple; I already gave it to you.

Walk with a mindfulness of what surrounds you. Be grateful for the sun beaming down on you, the destination you are going to, the shoes you are walking in and the air you are breathing. I promise you, those are not little things to millions of people in this world suffering. Be appreciative for all that you have, at all times.

With your mind set to gratitude, you will have the clarity to truly appreciate all that life has blessed you with. This mindset will allow you to be open to new opportunities, inspiration and creativity. Your relationships will flourish and your vision will come into focus. You want to get in this flow, and stay in this flow. You will be tuned into life in a new way, being able to feel the ways in which the universe is working for you.

Consistent gratitude will amplify your life and the greatness that is within you. Get out of the old mindset of magnifying the problems you face. Instead I challenge you to minimise any hardships solely by focusing on everything that brings you joy. I challenge you even further by thanking the hardships in your life, for the perspective and lessons they bring. Nothing is too small to be grateful for, nothing too big.

Be intentional in the life you want to create. You are the artist, the designer, the director in your life. You can cut the scene at any moment and bring in a blank canvas. Redirect that focus with your roots truly grounded in a place of full appreciation. Feel that inspiration, breathe in the greatness of the present moment and thank the universe for all that you are experiencing.

This is a lifestyle that will reward you constantly. And it will attract great people and things into your life. Who doesn't want to be around a happy, appreciative, inspired person? Create the abundance you deserve by emanating nothing less than amazing energy and truly feel the shift in your experiences.

CONCLUSION

As everything has an end, so this book is coming to an end and my thrust in this book is to help you in your journey to Get Rich. I am sure, if you follow all the things religiously that I have recommended, till the time you start reading this concluding note, you will have become a Money Magnet. You have now traversed the boundaries, limitations, inhibitions, restrictions, blocks and become an example of how this could happen.

But, here I have an important thing to share with you—do not make your success as a stick to beat anyone with. Accept it with gratitude towards the Almighty/nature and keep on making your tomorrows better than todays. Remember **you can be kind, loving, generous, healthy, spiritual and really filthy RICH.**

Getting rich with virtues, like compassion, warmth in relationship, sensitivity towards the problem of the people, appreciation for those who do good work, readiness to do something for the greater good or greater glory of the society and nation, so on and so forth gives a true sense of being Rich.

Relationship cannot be built overnight; health cannot be achieved in the wink of an eye. The attitudes of gratitude, help, etc. are the seeds that take time to germinate as well. And these are the important ingredients in the recipe of getting super rich.

So, to begin your Money Game, first of all define your purpose for which you want to Get Rich. Your purpose could be anything from enjoying the luxuries of life to living your passions to serving the masses. Whatever it is, you will need a lot of money to live your purpose to the fullest.

Now, you are on the right way to Get Rich this Year. You are no longer a person with limiting beliefs. You are now a bird. My chapters will become your wings and help you fly higher and higher in the horizon of abundance. Your wings will make you reach in the World of Richness this year itself.

Money is a tricky topic and sometimes you need handholding on your journey to Get Rich. So for the readers of my book, I offer a Money breakthrough session online which I normally charge thousands of rupees per session but offering free for you.

After reading the book, Rohan came for this 35 min online session and this is what he has to say, “This session has changed my view of money entirely - and for the better. I found the experience very encouraging and insightful. It was easy to follow, and made me look forward to a future of financial stability and comfort, where I feel like I can plan for a future. I also started making passive income which is a big relief for me."

Smita also came and this is what she has to say about the session, "I had quit my job and was struggling with debt as there was no savings in my new business. I realised that I was failing because I had a bad relationship with money. I had read all the books on money however still I couldn't get a breakthrough in money area. The session helped me to put a plan in place for saving money and paying off my debt."

If I can be of any help in your journey of getting rich then schedule your bonus money breakthrough session, let me help you make more money, this way I will be living my life's purpose and you can get rich this year. To schedule the session, please ✉ at harshhaagarg@gmail.com

Yours friendly Money Breakthrough Coach

–Harshhaa Garg

www.harshhaagarg.com